THE FINGER LAKES
of NEW YORK

THE FINGER LAKES
of NEW YORK

PHOTOGRAPHY BY CHARLES HARRINGTON

INTRODUCTION BY CAROL KAMMEN

Norfleet Press   New York

Published by
NORFLEET PRESS INC.
1133 Broadway
New York, New York 10010

Distributed by
NORTH COUNTRY BOOKS
311 Turner Street
Utica, New York 13501-1727
(315) 735-4877
Fax (315) 738-4342

FIRST EDITION

LIBRARY OF CONGRESS CATALOGING-IN-PUBLICATION DATA
Harrington, Charles, 1942-
       The Finger Lakes of New York / photography by Charles Harrington;
   introduction by Carol Kammen.
           p.   cm.
       Includes bibliographical references (p.139) and index.
       ISBN 0-9649934-0-6 (alk. paper). —ISBN 0-9649934-1-4 (pbk.: alk. paper)
       1. Finger Lakes (N. Y.)—Pictorial works.   2. Finger Lakes (N. Y.)—History.   I. Title.
   F127.F4H37   1996
   974.7′8—dc20   96-1332
                                                                                  CIP

Director & Producer: John G. Tucker
Designer: Abby Goldstein
Editor: Sabra Maya Feldman
Map designer: Wilhelmina Reyinga-Amrhein
1 2 3 4 5 6 7 8 9 10
Printed and bound in China

Frontispiece: Stone bridge from the 1930s spans the stream at Robert H. Treman State Park, Ithaca.

Contents

Introduction

☙ THE LAKE COUNTRY

In New York's lake country, past meets present. It is easy to believe that here, next to the up-to-date and modern, older patterns and values continue — that in some profound way, this region of the Finger Lakes is connected with a purer, better time.

It is not true, of course, or at least no more true here than anywhere else, but the region lulls us into believing that it might be so. Drive over a hill and suddenly there is a lake — appearing pristine, untouched, unadorned by the clutter of modern life. Could Iroquois be camped nearby? Is the steamboat due? Jog around a curve in the road and find a single farmhouse or barn and realize that this same vista could have been seen — was seen — a hundred years ago. Fly above the area and see spread out below the tapering lakes ("unequivocal exclamations," writes one poet) bounded by tree-covered hills. The land appears to stretch to the horizon unbroken, crisp, and new.

Myth, too, is close at hand amid the Finger Lakes. Folklore is commonplace and remnants of archaic speech are heard daily. Bizarre stories persist, contributing to the belief that we share a distinct local character.

The local past thrives in the Finger Lakes; it is known, it is lived with, and it is one of the area's charms for residents and visitors alike. Most people who travel here enjoy the experience of being "back there where the past was." Those of us who live here take for granted a world that encompasses contradictions. Blended here are ideas of what past times were and what modern times are, for in and around the Finger Lakes such collisions take place daily. Here vacation time and real life exist side by side, as do rocky cliffs and carefully cut stone walls, eagles flying free and Cornell's Laboratory of Ornithology, trillium sweeping down hillsides and experimental fields where grains to feed the world are developed.

The past coexists with the present; they abut each other, they merge: the historic and the modern, the real and the imagined, the folk and the scientific, the ideal and the real.

There are eleven lakes generally identified as Finger Lakes, a name for the region that only came into use at the end of the nineteenth century. Cayuga is the longest, measuring 38 miles from end to end; Seneca Lake is 36-and-a-half miles long and the deepest, at 634 feet. Their names come from those of two of the Iroquois tribes. The smallest lakes are at the edges of the area: the Pinkie Lakes, some call them — the little fingers. Some of their names can be traced to the descriptive Indian terms by which they were originally known. In the west there is Canadice, only three miles long but taking its name from a word for "long lake"; Honeoye, meaning "finger lying" or "where the finger lies," is five miles in length; Hemlock, named for the logging community that developed nearby, is eight miles long; Conesus is nine miles long, named, according to Arch Merrill, Gahn-yuh-sas from the sheep berries that grew on its shores. At the eastern edge of the region, Lake Otisco is six miles long. Its name comes from the Iroquoian word meaning "waters much dried away." Fifteen-mile-long Skaneateles's name means "long lake," although at one time romantics tried to tie it to the word for "beautiful maiden," — descriptively apt but not entymologically accurate. Owasco means "lake of the floating bridge" and is eleven miles long. In the center of the area are the three biggest lakes, Cayuga, Seneca, and Keuka (the latter twenty-two miles long and shaped like a 'Y'), and sixteen-mile-long Canandaigua, a name, according to Lewis Henry Morgan (a nineteenth-century anthropologist from Aurora), that means "place selected for settlement."

Seneca Lake has the reputation of being the fiercer of the two largest lakes. An Iroquois tale explained their different natures. A giant serpent once spanned the entire area that became New York, blocking the hunters' route to the north while allowing game to leap over its back and escape. During a starving time, a young brave strung a magic bow and pierced the serpent in its center. The creature flung itself into the air and split in two, its tail falling into Seneca Lake — which accounts for its turbulence — while the creature's head landed in Cayuga Lake — which explains its more placid, "thoughtful" character.

So deep are the two central Finger Lakes that since the nineteenth century stories have circulated about a dragon inhabiting their waters. Sometimes it was a fearsome thing, snake-like in form and threatening. At other times, especially recently, it is a benign creature much like a giant mermaid, who patrols the lake and has been seen by only a few. Divers who look for sunken barges are apt to circulate reports about encounters with this creature.

The depth of the lakes and their individual characteristics have fostered a number of other myths. The lakes are so deep and cold, some say, that the drowned do not reappear but are trapped below in the frigid waters. Cayuga Lake is reported to produce a booming sound called "lake drums." Legend explains that these sounds are made either by Revolutionary War soldiers drumming their way home from the colonial army's campaign against the Iroquois, or else that they signal lost lovers looking, endlessly looking, for each other among the hills. The sounds are heard in the spring and fall, when the air pressure is particularly low and a storm is approaching — a phenomenon known in only two other places on earth and identified as Barisol Drums. Lore serves as well as scientific truth, and the multiple explanations persist comfortably side by side. As a character in a play about local legends explains, "up here in the Lake Country we've lived with this business a *long* time . . . 'n while it's cert'nly mysteerious, it's a leetle something t' make life interestin'!"

Traditionalists believe that the lakes are connected, that between Seneca and Cayuga there is a secret tunnel through which objects can float. This is not true, declare the geologists, but the notion persists. Others say that the lakes foretell the weather. When the water turns green, sailors head for home. Even the fish in the lakes — small and largemouth bass, lake and rainbow trout, Atlantic salmon and perch — are imbued with myth: the story goes that one young man, leaning out of a boat, leaned so close to the water that an irate bass took a bite from his nose!

The Finger Lakes region is glacial terrain, covered by a salt sea millions of years ago. As the climate changed, the sea evaporated, leaving a layer of salt on land that was slowly swept and gouged by gigantic glaciers pushing down from Canada's Laurentian Range. The glaciers, two of them spaced ten thousand years apart, scraped out streams and rivers, and what had been minor depressions developed into lakes. Today the head of Cayuga Lake is at the south, the foot at its northern end, and the lake empties into the Lake Ontario water basin. The glacial activity buried the salt layer under several hundred feet of debris that forms the contours of the land. Salt is mined today by digging beneath Cayuga and Seneca lakes; we get road salt from one, table salt from the other. The mine beneath Cayuga Lake goes 2,300 feet below the surface and is the deepest rock-salt mine in North America.

The land around the lakes was cold and dank following the era of the glaciers, and it was inhospitable to human life. There are reports of woolly mammoths that roamed here, and a mammoth skeleton was exhumed in the town of Caroline. Only when hunters and gatherers appeared did people begin to leave traces on the land. Archaic hunters made temporary campsites at the marshy ends of the lakes and on Frontenac Island, the only island to be found in all of the Finger Lakes. Archeologists have found the charred remains of fires on Frontenac, a number of burial sites, some bone bundles, and grave

goods. At one time it was a fashionable sport to paddle out to the island to see what could be found; today Frontenac is protected by the state. It can be visited by boat from Union Springs, but nothing may be moved or carried away. The island is slightly under an acre in area and eight feet above the level of Cayuga Lake. It was formed during the Paleozoic Era by the run-off from a mainland stream that deposited silt against a coral reef.

The archaic people who moved about the Finger Lakes region lived at campsites so long as food and fuel were easily found; then they traveled on. They were followed by the Owasco People, who flourished from roughly 1000 to 1300 A.D. Skeletal remains show that the Owasco were of medium stature with long, narrow skulls; they were physically different from the archaic people who preceded them, and different, too, from the Iroquois who followed. The Owasco were New York's earliest cultivators of corn, beans, and squash. Hunting and fishing supplemented their diet. An Owasco site located in Emerson Park in Auburn is the place to learn more about these early residents.

The Iroquois came into the area early in the fourteenth century. They regarded the land on which they settled as the hand of the Great Spirit. Even though they could not observe the lakes from above to see their vivid finger-like configuration, the Iroquois understood and used the image of fingers when describing their home place, saying that they lived upon the hand of the Great Manitou. The Iroquois arrived in small groups, hostile to each other until the fifteenth-century develoment of the Great Confederation led by Deganawida and Hiawatha, who believed that in union the five tribes would be strong. In 1712, the confederacy took in Tuscarora Indians fleeing the expansion of white settlement in North Carolina. Then the Lake Country became known as the home of the Six Nations.

So strong did the Iroquois become during the seventeenth and eighteenth centuries that the British defined the borders of the land of the Iroquois Confederacy by treaty. Settlement by Europeans beyond the Unadilla River was prohibited. The territory was recognized by all as Iroquoia, the home of the Mohawks, Oneidas, Onondagas, Cayugas, Senecas, and Tuscaroras. They called themselves the Haudenosaunee — the "people of the longhouse."

Americans viewed the land of the Finger Lakes — Iroquoia — with alarm during the War for Independence, for it was from beyond the long, tapering lakes that Iroquois warriors and their English allies emerged to attack frontier settlements. As long as the domestic population was threatened, soldiers serving in the Continental Army were anxious when away from home. To protect New York's frontier settlements, and because other military maneuvers were too costly to mount, George Washington sent General John Sullivan into the Land of the Six Nations in 1779 with instructions to destroy the Iroquois Confederacy.

Sullivan's campaign along the Finger Lakes achieved little of military value, but as a real estate tour for the army it was overwhelmingly successful. Here before them men who were tenants, men who labored for others, men who farmed worn-out land saw pleasantly situated towns, grassy meadows, and, in the Iroquois fields and orchards, astonishing yields. General John Clark wrote that his regiment found "apples, peaches, Potatos, Tuyrnops, Onions, Pumpkins, Squashes, and Vegatablis of Various kinds in Great Plenty." The soldiers eyed the running streams, too, as power for mills. Some declared the "soyl very good." Although this was a military expedition, the army looked at the land through the eyes of farmers and millers and manufacturers — through the eyes of prospective settlers. Sergeant Thomas Roberts wrote that this was "the Best that Ever I see . . . Wee Marched through this Good Land 8 Mils." And Lieutenant Rudolphus Van Hovenburgh observed: "the Sight of the Sinnekic Lake as pretty a Lake as ever I Beheld and most beautiful land and it appeared to be very good Land on the other side of the Lake." The area's orchards, diary farms, and vineyards continue to send produce to market today.

At the end of the Revolutionary War, after the peace and a false start in the Adirondacks, the State of New York set aside 160 million acres of land in the heart of the Finger Lakes as a Military Tract to be used to pay off its debts to the soldiers who had fought without compensation during the war. The area was surveyed, mapped, and divided into towns. Those towns were divided again into parcels to be given to the veterans: the higher the rank, the greater the number of acres, with privates to receive 600 acres apiece. The land was not distributed until the early 1790s, however, some seven years after the soldiers had returned home from the war. During the interval, many of them had resumed their old lives or had created lives anew. For many of the veterans the land payment came too late, so they sold or traded it to others. Some of those who received parcels of land were swindled of their grants and some received unsatisfactory allocations, resulting in any number of lawsuits. Yet some veterans came west, along with other settlers, filling up the "new western lands" of central New York. A number of those original land grants remain intact to this day.

The land commissioners in Albany reached into the past to christen these new towns, peppering the region with classical names. So we can find Hannibal and Lysander, Camillus and Pompey for military men of the ancient world. There is Ulysses, too, named for the Greek wanderer, Homer for the blind poet, and Solon, the ancient lawgiver; Romulus was named for the founder of Rome (although there is no Remus). Dryden, Milton, and Locke recalled English writers. Some Iroquois words were retained, mostly to designate major land formations, and other sorts of names added. Some were those of the previous homes of settlers, like Groton or Enfield, in Connecticut; some were names that figured in current news stories, such as Chili, Lima, Warsaw, and Varna (a battlesite visited by Napoleon); some honored heroes, both local and national, such as Scott, Preble, Lafayette, and Fayette. Other names were descriptive. Residents called one community Etna because the local distillery sparked like a volcano. English visitors in particular scoffed at tiny communities loftily called Syracuse or Ithaca or Geneva. From this potpourri, the area became known as the Land of Silly Names.

As settlement increased from a trickle of pioneers in the 1790s to a steady flow of newcomers during the first two decades of the nineteenth century, many residents called the region the Land of Whiskey and Pumpkin Pie, indicating their origins and divisions. Some came from New England: people who believed in town meetings and taxation for education. They were the Pie People, mostly disapproving of those from the Middle Atlantic states — New York, Pennsylvania, and New Jersey — whose traditions were less inclined to public intervention in what they considered private concerns. Where the two groups converged, the populace was apt to be somewhat more rowdy than would have

been acceptable in Boston or Plymouth. Those from the Mid-Atlantic states tolerated alcohol and disdained their New England neighbors as "straight-laced" and puritanical. Contests between these mixed populations usually concerned the naming of a community. A New England name like Middlesex or Wayland was thought to frighten away settlers from the other camp. A name from the Middle Atlantic states was believed to indicate too loose a community foundation for those from the Bay State. At one settlement along Keuka Lake no name could be found to suit both groups. A fight was barely avoided when the residents agreed to compromise by selecting a name celebrating both traditions, calling it Pennsylvania-Yankee, or today, Penn Yan.

Few Iroquois remained in the area of the Finger Lakes after the Revolutionary War. Most of the Cayugas and Senecas departed for land granted to them in Canada. Some Iroquois settled on nine reservations agreed upon over a ten-year period of discussions with New York State officials. The Onondaga Reservation, located at Nedrow, south of Syracuse, is near the council fire of the old Confederation.

As the Iroquois moved out of the Finger Lakes, into it came a trickle of African-American settlers. Some received land grants in reward for their participation in the Revolutionary War, among them Primus Grant, called "the Guinea man," an early landowner in his corner of Cortland County, and Prince de Plessis, who settled in the Town of Danby in Tompkins County. Others came into central New York seeking asylum, looking for work, hoping to make new lives for themselves on the frontier, where skill and energy should matter more than race.

Survival, and then success, were common goals shared by all newcomers of the settling generation. They were farmers and millers, lawyers and doctors and laborers of all types. Preachers were numerous, since the clergy had no intention of allowing people to head for the frontier without the comforts of preaching and the cautions of organized religion.

Such intense religious fervor occurred in and around the Finger Lakes during the first third of the nineteenth century that the land became known as the Burned-Over District. Religious concerns flourished, new religions appeared, revivalism ran rampant. The land and the people were swept time and time again by religious enthusiasms. And such enthusiasms! There were millenialists, most notably the Millerites, those followers of Father William Miller who expected the world to end at a specific date and, when it did not, believed that a new calculation established a sure date for the following year. There were charismatic revivalists like William G. Finney and his squads of evangelists, who fanned out preaching about sin and the need for repentance. From this general religious ferment there also developed the Church of the Latter Day Saints — the Mormons.

There were utopians, too, people who believed that here was a place to restructure society. One of the earliest utopian leaders was Jemima Wilkinson, the self-styled Publick Universal Friend, who came to Seneca Lake in 1790 and then moved on with her two hundred followers to Keuka Lake. The Friend ruled her little community with skill, and her followers believed fervently in her claim that she had sickened, died, and arisen as the female form of Jesus Christ. When she declared that she could walk on water as Jesus of Nazareth had, her community gathered at the lake's edge to watch. The Friend approached the shore, turned and asked the congregation, "Do you believe that I can walk on water?" They eagerly agreed that they believed she could do such a thing. Well then, replied the Friend, in that case there was little need to do so, whereupon she turned on her heel and returned to her cottage. Undeterred, her followers continued to believe.

There were other communities reflecting the region's concern with social perfectionism. Shakers lived for a time in Wayne County, followed by Fourierists at the same site. There was a utopian community in Mottville that eschewed alcohol and tobacco and governmental control. Perfectionists gathered at the Oneida Community near Utica, scandalizing their neighbors with their belief in complex

marriage — in which there were no permanent unions — and eugenics. The Oneida Community ended as a profitable silver company. There were also the followers, even if they were but few, of Cyrus Reed Teed, a dabbler in electricity. When he was shocked by too much current from an experiment in his laboratory, he believed that he had died and been transformed into a new incarnation of God. He took a new name, calling himself Koresh, the Hebrew form of Cyrus, and formed a religion known as Kore-shanty. He gathered converts from all over the Finger Lakes area who believed that they were living, not on the outside of the earth from which they would surely fall off, but on the inside. Koreshanty moved to the west coast of Florida and lasted well into the 1950s.

Central New York was crossed by any number of itinerant preachers and revivalists who stirred people up and left them exhausted and perhaps no closer to God, but agitated nonetheless about their eternal salvation. Ithaca, a community with a ribald early history, so sordid that the earliest settlement was called briefly Sodom and Sin City, was by the late 1820s a village where "religion was talked on every street corner." Preaching billowed out of Ithaca's churches and could be heard, it was said, from several blocks away.

The Lake Country was a land of religious enthusiasm, but it was also, for a time, a place where you could hear the hum of enterprise as towns and hamlets attempted to develop products that would bring them fame and prosperity. All sought connections to outside markets, for even at an early date people realized that this area was relatively remote from commerce and that isolation threatened economic stagnation. Towns competed with each other for the benefits of progress. Ithaca was connected to southern markets by a toll road to Owego; Watkins Glen won the rights to a canal to the south.

At one time, fast-running streams powered small factories that turned out woolen goods, lumber, and paper. Later iron bridges were made here, and typewriters, but the industrial consolidation of the late nineteenth and early twentieth centuries forced many companies to close, while the economic conditions of the recent past have caused others to change or move away. Today, the Lake Country is predominantly rural in nature, but dotted with several small cities — Auburn, Geneva, Elmira, Canandaigua, Skaneateles, Ithaca — none with a population greater than 34,000.

Methodists selected Ithaca as the site of a college to be built on East Hill to educate both men and women. Then the church officials changed their minds and settled their institution in Cazenovia. To counter the loss, Ithaca's promoters established an academy of their own. Printing enterprises in Geneva and Ithaca competed with each other. Auburn became the home of the state prison, and from that institution evolved the Auburn system of penology: prisoners were kept in separate cells, they were identified by number rather than name, they wore striped clothing to denude them of individuality, they lived according to the iron precision of the clock, and they worked in prison enterprises to earn their keep and to keep them occupied. So famous was the Auburn prison that travelers heading to Niagara Falls would stop and pay a quarter to see the prisoners go through their paces.

In the early years of the nineteenth century, people lived in crudely made cabins. When milled lumber became available, residents constructed houses in the Federal style. By 1830, however, the dominant architectural form throughout the region was the Greek or Classical Revival. Major public buildings and churches in the centers of towns were built with tall white pillars, triangular pediments, and stately doorways, giving them a serene dignity. The area became identified with such houses, homes to match the names that had already been put upon the land. Later architectural styles would appeal to some, and people built Italianate and Gothic Revival homes to follow then-current architectural fashions, but the older Greek Revival houses were maintained, still punctuating and defining the landscape to this day. Nowadays such historic homes are interspersed with modern structures, some of them of stunning originality.

Central New York blossomed, not with industrial enterprises as expected, but with perfectionist movements. Here, abolition and temperance became important causes. It was to small, central New York communities in the Finger Lakes region that Harriet Tubman led many of the African Americans she brought forth from slavery. In Rochester, of course, Frederick Douglass found a home and published his newspaper, *The North Star*. Escaped slaves headed through central New York, enlarging the African-American communities in Elmira and Auburn, Geneva and Ithaca. In Seneca Falls, Elizabeth Cady Stanton and her colleagues launched the Women's Rights movement in 1848 with a convention held in the Methodist Chapel. Today, the Women's Rights National Historical Park and the National Women's Hall of Fame are located in Seneca Falls.

Educational innovation also flourished in the region of the Finger Lakes. Several towns had fine academies where children of both genders received classical educations along with training in music and art — but, as one academy advertised, the practical subjects were taught first. For a time, young men wishing further education needed to leave the Finger Lakes. They went to Union College in Schenectady, or to universities founded before the American Revolution, such as Columbia University in New York City, or Yale or Princeton. Collegiate education for women began in 1853 when Elmira College opened. Cornell University opened in 1868, created with Morrill Land Grant monies and dedicated to the education of farmers and mechanics. But the university also offered a rigorous classical education, allowing students a choice of studies. In 1872, Cornell opened its doors to women.

In the literature of the region, *David Harum* and *Tess of the Storm Country* are preeminent. David Hannum of Homer, the model for the fictional Harum, was a kindly local character who hid his philanthropy beneath a crusty exterior. Harum was a Homer banker and horse trader who was supposed to have warned, "Do unto others what they would do unto you, and do it furst!" He was the man who in 1869 engineered the planting of the Cardiff Giant, the supposedly ancient, petrified remains of a giant that fooled many. P. T. Barnum, the circusman, created a copy that proved to be a money-maker. The original Giant can be visited in Cooperstown today, a century after the book about Harum became a best-seller.

Grace Miller White, author of *Tess of the Storm Country*, created a cast of memorable characters in her novels set in the Finger Lakes region. Her books feature heroines of humble origins — Tess and Judy and Rose and Polly — along with petty pastors and devious lawyers. In their day, White's books were universally popular and several became motion pictures; today, these books are sought by collectors. Writers of fiction, poetry, and drama, as well as artists of all sorts , now live in the Lake Country, among them winners of both the Pulitzer and Nobel prizes. Ithaca is known to have a greater number of bookstores than many larger cities. The performing arts are also alive and well, with theater and dance companies, choirs, bands, and orchestras throughout the Lake Country.

Central New York has long been home to visual artists, too, dating from Henry Walton's stay in the area in the 1830s, when he painted portraits and created views of Ithaca and Elmira. In the second decade of the twentieth century, Ithaca was the home of a fledgling movie industry. *The Mysteries of*

Myra was filmed locally, and so were background sequences that appeared in the *Perils of Pauline* and other serials. By 1920, however, that industry had fled to sunnier climates where outdoor filming was possible year round.

The automobile transformed life in the Finger Lakes, opening it up to vacationers from afar, who viewed it as an idyllic retreat. Cottages appeared along the lakes and summer visitors became as much a part of the routine of the year as the geese who noisily returned each spring from the south. Cars and their fragile tires required that area roads be improved and tourist facilities increased. There was no way, however, to link all the lakes by one modern turnpike, so travel in the region continues to this day to follow the lakes' contours. Only early in the nineteenth century was there a bridge in the Finger Lakes, a wooden span that crossed the marshy northern end (or foot) of Cayuga Lake.

The idea of region is difficult to define. In the case of the Lake Country, one definition places boundaries that another contradicts: so it is with Iroquoia, the Military Tract, the Land of Silly Names, the Burned-Over District, the Inland Empire, the Storm Country. None of these designations denote the same area, yet all are descriptive of this place. The contours of the Lake Country include farm and factory, urban and rural communities, affluence and hard-scrabble poverty, progressive and conservative ways of life; the area expands and contracts to suit individual tastes. At times, workers in high-tech companies look out at acres of trellised grape vines or family farms.

The core, the defining heart, of the area, however, is the lakes themselves — long, tapering, graceful. Their names roll off the tongue and conjure images both vivid and distant: Otisco, Skaneateles, Owasco, Cayuga, Seneca, Keuka, Canandaigua, Honeoye, Canadice, Hemlock, Conesus. They echo things half-known, half-remembered, calling to mind a past before historic time when there were no demarcations on the land. The lakes remind us of a time when the area was newly made, when glaciers receded to reveal fingers upon the land.

The Finger Lakes retain their mystery. They are seen mostly in glimpses, rarely in their entirety, and their moods take many years to know. We catch pieces of them — moments of blue or green water as we drive along their shores — but much is unseen. To many, the lakes look like rivers because they stretch out beyond our view. They are not always calm, nor are they always benign. Their moods are felt by those well back on the shore as well as those on the water. The lakes remain, even after long acquaintance, an unpredictable, unknowable presence.

Today, above all, the Lake Country evokes images of recreation — of boating and swimming, of hiking along the irregular shores. Evoked, too, are images of creation — students and ideas flowing from the colleges and universities, wine from the vineyards, new technology from the many small companies, and works of art from studios and hideaways. All this activity takes place within an ever-changing landscape: the palest greens of a newly blossoming spring, the clarity of light on a summer's day, the brilliant multicolors of fall, the bite of the air after a winter snow.

The Lake Country is a destination for many, but to get to the Finger Lakes is to make a considerable journey in time as well as space. The Greek writer C. P. Cavafy thought the importance of "Ithaki" was the trip one took to get there, and so it was for Ulysses, who spent twenty years finding his way home. The Cornell graduate and writer E. B. White wrote that central New York was a place one got to — and stayed — because access and egress were made only with difficulty.

Today, being in the Lake Country, or being of it, is important in itself. Visitors and residents alike are enveloped by its history, its lore, its promise. In the Lake Country, past meets present, ideal meets reality. It is, residents proudly proclaim in their crustiest manner, the most centrally isolated place in the East.

CAROL KAMMEN
Ithaca, New York

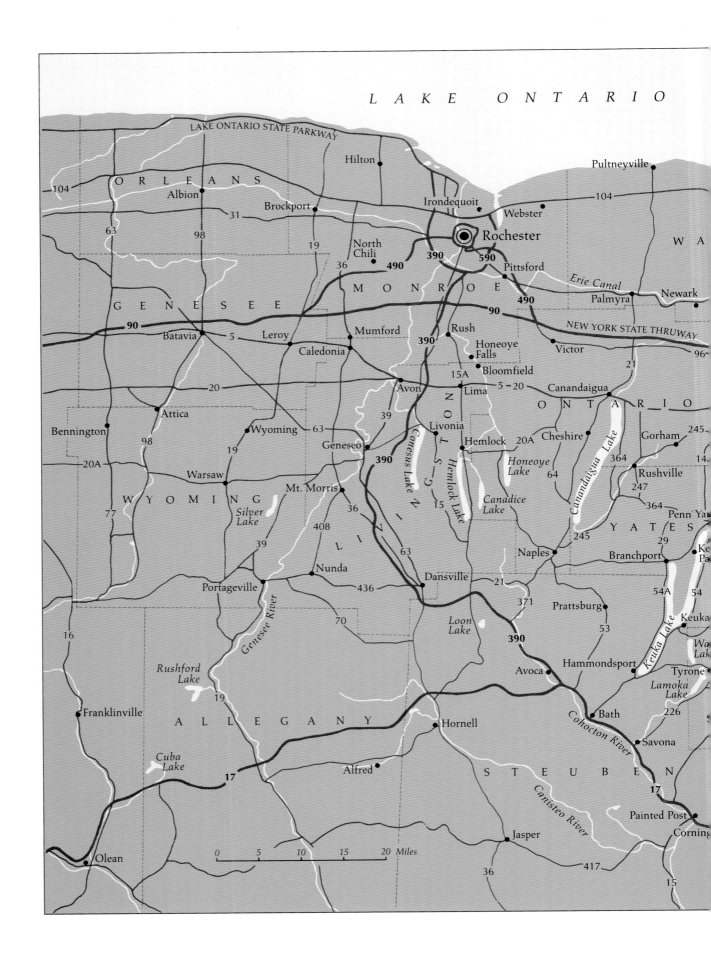

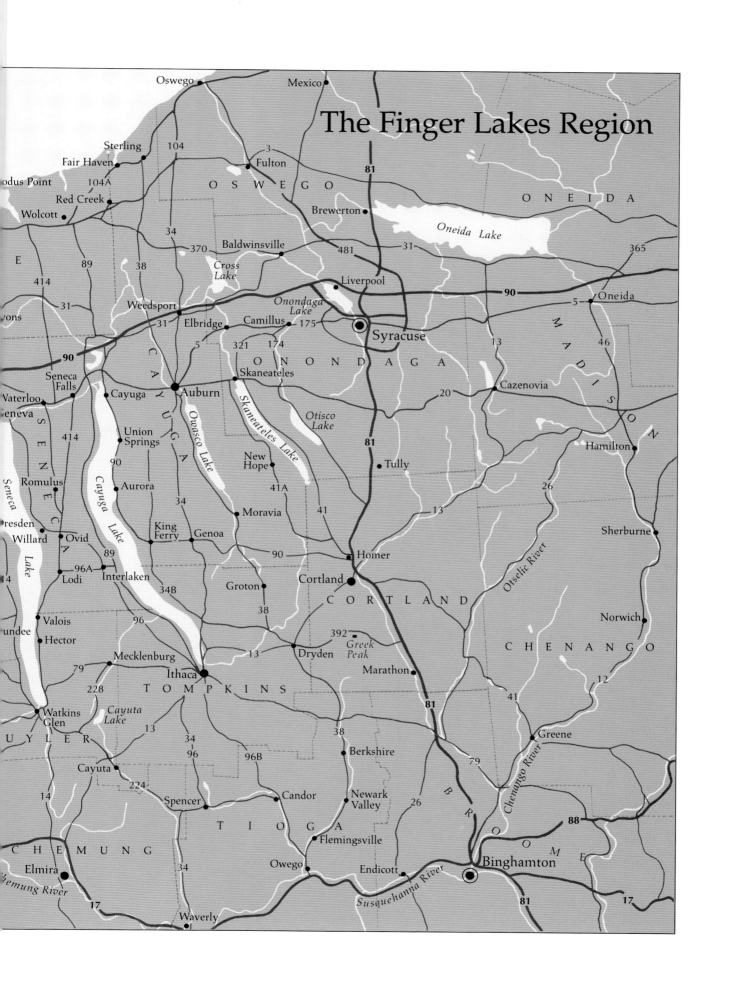

The Finger Lakes Region

Vineyard overlooking Seneca Lake near Hector, Schuyler County.

Montezuma National Wildlife Refuge, at the foot of Cayuga Lake, contains 6,000 acres of varied habitat, including extensive marshes, and is an important link in the North American flyway.

A wide variety of shorebirds can be found in the Finger Lakes region, including eleven species of gulls.
These gulls are at the lakeshore park in Geneva.

Spiked teasel heads were once used to brush and raise the nap on cloth.

October wildflowers near Ovid, Seneca County.

Silo and barn near Varick, Seneca County.

Grapevines overlooking east side of Seneca Lake.

Rolled hay near East Bloomfield, Ontario County.

Corn crib in Genoa, Cayuga County. As summer bounty and winter feed,
corn has long been an important crop in the region.

Sheep on a farm near Fayette, Seneca County.

*Farm in Varick. Dairy farms and orchards have replaced much of the
original grain crops of the Finger Lakes region.*

Haying on a farm in East Bloomfield. Farming remains an important way of life throughout the area.

During the 1970s, a number of Protestant sectarians moved onto Seneca County farms.
This gathering of Mennonite women is in the town of Fayette.

Amish men build a roof in Fayette.

Gable-roofed barns predominante in the region; this one is in Bloomfield.

Fall pumpkin crop from the King Farm, Seneca County.

Farm in East Bloomfield, Ontario County.

Draft horses kept by Amish farmers, Fayette.

Harness display at the Granger Homestead and Carriage Museum, Canandaigua.

In the picturesque village of Skaneateles, Onondaga County, this nineteenth-century grist mill is now a restaurant.

Community park in the village of Skaneateles overlooks Skaneateles Lake.

Summer swimming in Cayuga Lake.

The first steamboat sailed on Cayuga Lake in 1821.
Today, recreational uses such as sailing and
sail boarding predominate.

Alan H. Treman State Marine Park in Ithaca,
New York State's only inland marina.

Columbia *cruises the length of Seneca Lake, leaving from the marina at Watkins Glen.*

Judge Ben Wiles *sails twice a day from Skaneateles, where the mail packet is still in operation.*

From atop almost any ridge, there is a lake in the distance. This view overlooks Keuka Lake from the west.

Cayuga Lake near Seneca Falls.

Midsummer at the Canandaigua Marina.

Placing flares along the southern shore of Cayuga Lake is a local tradition each Independence Day.

*Roof detail of the Rockwell Museum, a Romanesque Revival building
that was formerly Corning's City Hall.*

Clock tower, Auburn.

Fire station clock tower, 1911, Owego, Tioga County.

Interior of the Morgan Opera House, built in 1890 and still an active community theater in Aurora.

Italianate house dating to 1856 in Union Springs, Cayuga County.

The tallest Civil War monument in New York state, in Bloomfield.

Stoneware crocks at The Collection, Trumansburg.

*The amber color of these glass objects, displayed at the Caroline
Town Hall, was produced by their immersion in the mineral-laden waters of
Slaterville Springs, a practice that continues to this day.*

Cooking implements, Seneca Falls Historical Society.

*In the nineteenth century, many structures in the Finger Lakes were built of cobblestone,
a durable material. This cobblestone house is near Bloomfield.*

Old wooden farm cart and nineteenth-century barn with "Carpenter Gothic" trim in Trumansburg, Tompkins County.

Old barn, Tompkins County.

*Trophy wall of antlers in Lansing,
Tompkins County.*

Ontario County Court House, built 1858, Canandaigua.

Clock tower of Canandaigua City Hall, built in 1824.

Trinity Episcopal Church of Seneca Falls, built in 1885.

Geneva on the Lake was originally built in 1915 as a family residence. From 1948 to 1974, it was the home of the Capuchin Fathers, a Roman Catholic religious order, and is now a resort.

Sonnenberg Gardens, Canandaigua, Ontario County.

Pettibone House, built in 1857 in the Gothic Revival style, at Wells College in Aurora.

The Trumansburg Conservatory of Fine Arts, a Greek Revival structure built circa 1830.

In 1830, the Greek Revival-style Clinton House in Ithaca became one of the finest hotels in the state. It is now home to the local preservation society and arts agencies.

Late nineteenth-century Italianate villa, Ithaca.

Stained glass window from 1890 at the Cayuga Museum in Auburn.

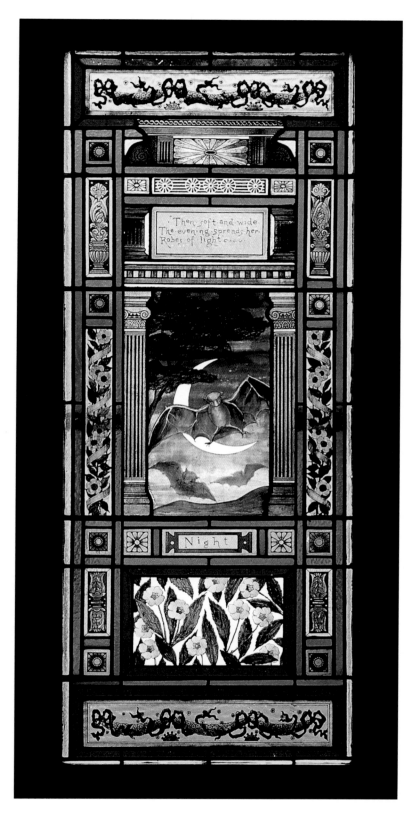

"Night," from a set of three stained glass windows at the Seneca Falls Historical Society.

The Stanton Gallery at the Cayuga Museum in Auburn.

Music Room at Rose Hill, a Greek Revival-style house built in 1839 overlooking Seneca Lake.

Nineteenth-century "Carpenter Gothic" house, Canandaigua.

Solarium in The 1890 House on Tompkins Street, Cortland.

Gothic-style bargeboards frame a dormer window on a circa 1870 house in Trumansburg.

Staircase at the Rose Inn, Lansing. The house was built in 1848 in the Italianate style; the stairs were added in 1924.

Garden behind William Henry Seward's Federal-style house in Auburn. Seward was President Lincoln's Secretary of State and is credited with the purchase of Alaska.

Old-fashioned pump organ at the Seneca Falls Historical Society.

Dining room in the Memorial Day Museum, Waterloo, built in 1830.

Detail of spool-decorated house built in 1895 in Hammondsport.

Samuel Langhorne Clemens's (a. k. a. Mark Twain) study, octagonal in the style of a Mississippi riverboat pilothouse, is on the campus of Elmira College, Elmira Heights.

Federal-style row houses constructed during the first twenty years of the nineteenth century, along Routes 5 and 20 in Geneva.

Limestone residence in Aurora, built in 1840 and purchased in 1864 by Henry Wells, founder of Wells Fargo, to serve as the town's bank.

Covered bridge dating to 1853 in Newfield, Tompkins County.

1880 Silsby fire engine, made in Seneca Falls, at the Seneca Falls Historical Society.

Antique cars at the Vintage Auto Museum, Watkins Glen.

Junebug, an early experimental plane at the Glen H. Curtis Museum, Hammondsport.

Memorial Day parade in Waterloo, Seneca County. Waterloo is the birthplace of Memorial Day, which commemorates those who died in the Civil War.

Memorial Day Museum, Waterloo.

Renaissance Fair occurs every August in Sterling.

Dragon Day, celebrated each March at Cornell University, pits architecture students against engineers, during which a dragon—representing winter—is burned.

Summer fair in Caroline, Tompkins County.

Early summer morning at The Store at Treman's Village, Trumansburg.

Gothic Revival Methodist church, built 1880, is now home to the Lodi Historical Society, Seneca County.

Taughannock State Park, Tompkins County.

Millpond near New Hope Mills in New Hope, Cayuga County.

The Corning Museum of Glass contains outstanding examples of glass-making from antiquity to the present. There is also an exhibit on glass technology as well as demonstrations of glass blowing and other techniques. The museum's collection includes a cut-glass boat (above) designed for Baccarat by the sculptor Charles Vital Cornu, 1851-1927, and an acid-etched punch bowl set (opposite) designed for the Paris Exposition Universelle of 1867.

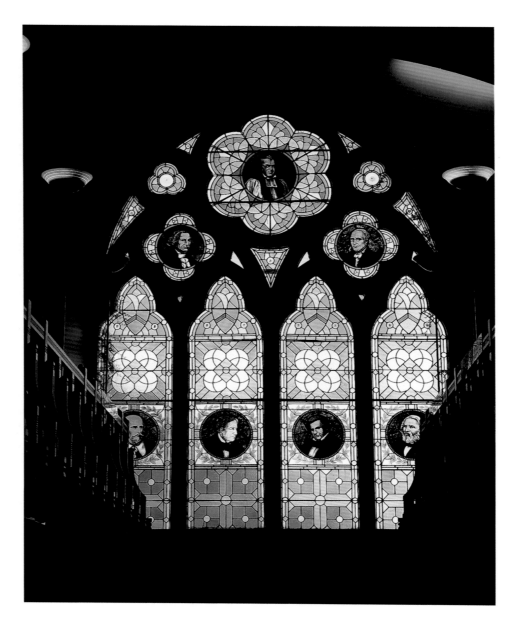

Stained-glass window of St. John's Chapel, located on the campus of Hobart and William Smith Colleges, Geneva. The Gothic Revival chapel (opposite) was built of Waterloo limestone in the 1860s.

Woodlawn National Cemetery in Elmira contains the graves of more than 3,000 Confederate soldiers.

Old stone ruins, Reynoldsville, on the edge of the Finger Lakes National Forest, Schuyler County.

Taughannock Falls in Tompkins County is the second highest waterfall east of the Rockies.

A fisherman casts for trout and bass at the base of Ithaca Falls.

Stone bridge from the 1930s near the entrance to Watkins Glen State Park.

Stone bridge at Robert H. Treman State Park, south of Ithaca.

Waterfall, Watkins Glen State Park.

Ithaca Falls.

Cooling off on Taughannock Creek's flat rocks in Trumansburg.

Hemlock Falls on the Onondaga Indian Reservation.

Shallow falls along hiking trail at Taughannock Falls State Park

Summertime at the bottom of the falls in Buttermilk Falls State Park, Ithaca.

McGraw Library Tower, built in 1893, is a familiar symbol of Cornell University in Ithaca.

Robinson York State Herb Garden, Cornell University.

Coxe Hall, built in 1900, houses the administrative offices of Hobart and William Smith Colleges, Geneva.

Mosaic and stained glass windows in Cornell University's Sage Chapel, erected in the 1870s.

Main Building at Wells College, Aurora, features a Romanesque Revival bell tower erected in 1889.

The Ithaca College campus overlooks Cayuga Lake.

Cross-country skiing is a popular winter sport around the Finger Lakes.

Ski lift at Greek Peak, Virgil, Cortland County.

Chequaga Falls, in the community of Montour Falls in Schuyler County,
is 156 feet high and located in the village center.

Winter view along the Tioughnioga River, Marathon, Cortland County.

Grapes ripen in the vineyards along Seneca Lake. Grape-growing and winemaking is a major Finger Lakes industry.

The Finger Lakes most illustrious winery building is this one, built for the Columbia Wine Company in 1880 in Hammondsport. The nation's first licensed winery was founded on this site in 1860.

Fox Run Vineyards, near Penn Yan, overlooks Seneca Lake.

The vineyards of Dr. Konstantin Frank's Vinifera Wine Cellars are on Keuka Lake.
Dr. Frank was a pioneering Finger Lakes winemaker.

Old wine casks, Hammondsport.

Stainless steel wine tanks at Glenora Wine Cellars, a Seneca Lake winery near Dundee.

Wagner Vineyards, established 1947, overlooks Seneca Lake.

Chardonnay grapes destined for one of the some fifty wineries located in the Finger Lakes region.

The modern building housing Lamoreaux Landing Wine Cellars, overlooking Seneca Lake, evokes an ancient Greek temple.

Spires of Crouse College of Visual & Performing Arts at Syracuse University.

Malvina Hoffman's 1936 statue, Elemental Man, *stands before the Dorothea Ilgen-Shaffer Art Building, Syracuse University.*

Baseball fans have been coming to MacArthur Stadium in Syracuse since 1934.

Contemporary mural in Manhattan Square Park, Rochester.

Gardens outside the George Eastman House, Rochester, housing the renowned International Museum of Photography and Film.

Rush-Rhees Library, built 1930, at the University of Rochester.

Stained glass window, 1905, by Louis Comfort Tiffany at the Corning Museum of Glass.

Selected Bibliography

Becker, Carl L., *Cornell University: Founders and the Founding*, Ithaca, 1943

Bishop, Morris, *A History of Cornell*, Ithaca, 1962

Carmer, Carl, *Listen for a Lonesome Drum: A York State Chronicle*, New York, 1936

——, *Dark Trees to the Wind: A Cycle of York State Years*, New York, 1949

Champlin, Charles, *Back There Where the Past Was: A Small-Town Boyhood*, Syracuse, 1989

Cross, Whitney R,. *The Burned-Over District*, New York, 1950

Dieckmann, Jane M., *A Short History of Tompkins County*, Ithaca, 1986

Drummond, A. M. and Gard, Robert E., *The Lake Guns of Seneca and Cayuga*, Ithaca, 1942

Ellis, David M., *et al., A History of New York State*, Ithaca, 1967

Fitchen, Janet M., *Poverty in Rural America: A Case Study*, Boulder, Colo., 1981

Kammen, Carol, *The Peopling of Tompkins County: A Social History*, Interlaken, 1985

——, *Lives Passed: Biographical Sketches from Central New York*, Interlaken, 1984

——, ed., *One Day in Ithaca: May 17, 1988*, Ithaca, 1989

Merrill, Arch., *Slim Fingers Beckon*, New York, n.d.

——, *The Lakes Country*, New York, 1944

Ritchie, William A. . *The Archaeology of New York State*, Garden City, 1969

Sisler, Carol U., *Cayuga Lake: Past, Present, and Future*, Ithaca, 1989

Sneller, Anne Gertrude , *A Vanished World*, Syracuse, 1964, 1994 reprint

Tall, Deborah, *From Where We Stand: Recovering a Sense of Place*, New York, 1993

Thompson, Harold W., *Body, Boots & Britches*, Philadelphia, 1940

Thompson, John H., ed., *Geography of New York State*, Syracuse, 1966

von Engeln, O. D., *The Finger Lakes Region: Its Origin and Nature*, Ithaca, 1961

Westcott, Edward N., *David Harum*, New York, 1898, 1960 reprint

White, Grace Miller, *Tess of the Storm Country*, New York, 1909

——, *Judy of Rogues' Harbor*, New York, 1918

——, *The Secret of the Storm Country*, New York, 1916

——, *The Shadow of the Sheltering Pines*, New York, 1919

Finger Lakes Reference

☞ STATE PARKS

Braddock Bay, Rochester · Buttermilk Falls, Ithaca · Cayuga Lake, Seneca Falls · Clark Reservation, Syracuse · Fair Haven Beach, Fair Haven · Fillmore Glen, Moravia · Green Lakes, Fayetteville · Hamlin, Hamlin · Keuka Lake, Penn Yan · Letchworth, Castile · Lodi Point, Lodi · Long Point, Aurora · Newtown Battlefield, Elmira · Pinnacle, Addison · Sampson, Romulus · Seneca Lake, Geneva · H. H. Spencer, Tabors Corners · Stony Brook, Dansville · Taughannock Falls, Ithaca · Allan H. Treman, Ithaca · Robert H. Treman, Ithaca · Watkins Glen, Watkins Glen

☞ HISTORIC SITES OF SPECIAL INTEREST

Susan B. Anthony Home, Rochester · Prouty-Chew Museum, Geneva · 1890 House, Cortland · Millard Fillmore Log Cabin Site, Moravia · Rose Hill Mansion, Geneva · Memorial Day Museum, Waterloo · Ganondagan State Historic Site, Victor · Gideon Granger Homestead and Carriage Museum, Canandaigua · Newtown Battlefield State Reservation, Elmira · Owasco Stockaded Indian Village, Auburn · Narcissa Prentiss House, Prattsburg · William Henry Seward House, Auburn · Joseph Smith Home, Palmyra · Elizabeth Cady Stanton Home, Seneca Falls · Harriet Tubman Home, Auburn · Mark Twain Study, Elmira · Women's Hall of Fame, Seneca Falls · Women's Rights National Park, Seneca Falls · Woodlawn Cemetery, Elmira

☞ MAJOR MUSEUMS

Alling Coverlet Museum, Palmyra · Arnot Art Museum, Elmira · Burnet Park Zoo, Syracuse · Cayuga Museum of History and Art, Auburn · Cornell Plantations, Ithaca · Corning Museum of Glass, Corning · Discovery Center of Science and Technology, Syracuse · Erie Canal Museum, Syracuse · Everson Museum of Art, Syracuse · Glen H. Curtiss Museum of Local History, Hammondsport · Genesee Country Museum, Mumford · Handwerker Gallery at Ithaca College, Ithaca · International Museum of Photography at George Eastman House, Rochester · Herbert F. Johnson Museum of Art at Cornell University, Ithaca · Memorial Art Gallery of the University of Rochester, Rochester · Memorial Day Museum, Waterloo · National Soaring Museum, Elmira · New York Museum of Transportation, Rochester · Rochester Museum of Science Center, Rochester · The Rockwell Museum, Corning · Sainte Marie Among the Iroquois Museum, Liverpool · Salt Museum, Liverpool · Sapsucker Woods Bird Sanctuary, Ithaca · Schweinfurth Art Center, Auburn · The Sciencenter, Ithaca · Sonnenberg Gardens and Mansion, Canandaigua · Margaret Woodbury Strong Museum, Rochester · Tioga Transportation Museum, Flemingville · Victorian Doll Museum, North Chili · Watkins Glen Racing Museum · Women's Hall of Fame, Seneca Falls · Women's Rights National Historical Park, Seneca Falls

FOUR-YEAR COLLEGES AND UNIVERSITIES

College of Environmental Science and Forestry, Syracuse (1911) · Cornell University, Ithaca (1865) · Eastman School of Music, Rochester (1921) · Elmira College, Elmira Heights (1853) · Hobart and William Smith Colleges, Geneva (1822 and 1908) · Ithaca College, Ithaca (1892) · Keuka College, Keuka Park (1890) · Le Moyne College, Syracuse (1946) · Nazareth College, Rochester (1924) · New York State University College at Brockport (1842) · New York State University at Cortland (1863) · Roberts Wesleyan College, North Chili (1866) · Rochester Institute of Technology, Rochester (1829) · Saint John Fisher College, Rochester (1952) · University of Rochester, Rochester (1850) · Syracuse University, Syracuse (1849) · Wells College, Aurora (1868)

COMMUNITY COLLEGES

Cayuga County Community College, Auburn · Corning Community College, Corning · Community College of the Finger Lakes, Canandaigua · Monroe Community College, Rochester · Onondaga Community College, Syracuse · Tompkins Cortland Community College, Dryden

WINERIES

Amberg Wine Cellars, Clifton Springs · Americana Vineyards, Interlaken · Anthony Road Wine Company, Penn Yan · Arbor Hill Grapery, Naples · Arcadian Estate Winery, Rock Stream · Batavia Wine Cellars, Batavia · Bully Hill Vineyards, Hammondsport · Canandaigua Wine Company, Canandaigua · Casa Larga Vineyards, Fairport · Cascata Winery, Watkins Glen · Castel Grisch Estate Winery, Watkins Glen · Cayuga Ridge Estate Vineyard, Ovid · Château LaFayette Reneau, Hector · Dr. Frank's Vinifera Wine Cellars, Hammondsport · Eagle Crest Vineyards, Conesus · Four Chimneys Farm Winery, Himrod · Fox Run Vineyards, Penn Yan · Frontenac Point Vineyard, Trumansburg · Fulkerson Winery, Dundee · Glenora Wine Cellars, Dundee · Hazlitt 1852 Vineyards, Hector · Hermann J. Wiemer Vineyard, Dundee · Heron Hill Vineyards, Hammondsport · Hosmer Winery, Ovid · Hunt Country Vineyards, Branchport · Keuka Spring Vineyards, Penn Yan · King Ferry Winery (Treleaven), King Ferry · Knapp Vineyards, Romulus · Lakeshore Winery, Romulus · Lakewood Vineyards, Watkins Glen · Lamoreaux Landing Wine Cellars, Lodi · Leidenfrost Vineyards, Hector · Lucas Vineyards, Interlaken · McGregor Vineyard, Dundee · New Land Vineyard, Geneva · Olde Germania Wine Cellars, Hammondsport · Pleasant Valley Wine Company, Hammondsport · Poplar Ridge Vineyards, Valois · Prejean Winery, Penn Yan · Rolling Vineyards, Hector · Signore Winery, Brooktondale · Silver Thread Vineyard, Trumansburg · Six Mile Creek Vineyard, Ithaca · Squaw Point Winery, Dundee · Standing Stone Vineyards, Valois · Swedish Hill Vineyard, Romulus · Thorpe Vineyard, Wolcott · Wagner Vineyards, Lodi · Widmer's Wine Cellars, Naples

Index

Acknowledgments

☞ *To those who contributed generously to this book, in ways both tangible and intangible:*

Lynn Carroll, David F. DeMarco, Sabra Maya Feldman, Abby Goldstein, Yuhong Guo
Karyl Hammond, Russell & Hester Hamilton, Joan Harrington, James Owen Mathews, Howard Musk
Barry Perlus, Heather Picken, Harry Tipton, Gladys Hartz Tucker, Iren Tucker

Special thanks to Susan Buckley Harrington from her devoted husband Charles.

☞ *In Memoriam*

Lawrence Bothwell, Janis Lee Cochran, Morrison Graham Tucker